Current African Issues No 68

Taxation for Inclusive Development

Challenges Across Africa

Written by
Jörgen Levin

NORDISKA AFRIKAINSITUTET
The Nordic Africa Institute
UPPSALA 2021

Indexing terms:

Taxation
Tax revenues
Tax systems
Income tax
Corporate tax
Public finance
Poverty alleviation
Social welfare
Africa

Taxation for Inclusive Development
Current African Issues No 68

© Nordiska Afrikainstitutet/The Nordic Africa Institute, 2021

Edited by
Jörgen Levin

ISSN 0280-2171
ISBN 978-91-7106-875-0   print-on-demand version
ISBN 978-91-7106-876-7   pdf e-book

THE NORDIC AFRICA INSTITUTE (Nordiska Afrikainstitutet) is a centre for research,
knowledge, policy advice and information on Africa. Based in Uppsala, Sweden,
we are a government agency, funded jointly by Sweden, Finland and Iceland.

The opinions expressed in this volume are those of the author and
do not necessarily reflect the views of the Nordic Africa Institute.

Print editions are available for purchase, more information can be found at the NAI
web page www.nai.uu.se.

Cover photo: Saleswoman in
Kawa General shop in Kericho,
Kenya. Photo: Corrie Wingate.

Contents

Introduction   6

Financing for Development   10

How Much Tax Revenue Do Countries Collect?   16

Taxing Firms   32

Taxing Individuals   42

Redistribution: The Role of Taxation and Public Spending   52

Conclusions and Recommendations   62

References   65

Appendix 1: ISO Codes and Countries   70

Introduction

The 2030 Agenda for Sustainable Development identifies a number of important targets aimed at improving living conditions globally. The situation is particularly acute in many low-income countries, especially across sub-Saharan Africa, where a large share of the population lacks access to such basic services as education, health and infrastructure. While advancements have been made towards the Sustainable Development Goals (SDGs), the COVID-19 pandemic is expected to slow progress. To address this, a scaling up of social protection programmes is urgently needed. Though in the short term aid is likely to be the major source of funding, over time African governments must invest in their fiscal capacity in order to mobilise domestic resources. In exploring this issue, the report focuses on SDG 17 – the strengthening of domestic resource mobilisation – and how it relates to SDG 10 (inequality) and SDG 1 (poverty).

In November 2019, the Nordic Africa Institute (NAI) organised a workshop on taxation involving approximately 25 participants and 20 presentations. Although the topics of the presentations varied, three broad themes were discussed: 1) taxation from the broader perspective of development finance; 2) compliance, ranging from cross-country studies to individual case studies; 3) taxation and inequality, ranging from a taxation and public-spending perspective to a spatial perspective.

The topics addressed in this report are framed around these workshop discussions, with the overarching question being how African governments can mobilise additional tax revenue in support of an inclusive development agenda. The report, which is based on a selective literature review combined with empirical analysis utilising the UNU-WIDER Government Revenue Dataset,[1] is divided into six chapters. Chapter 1 discusses the role of taxation

---

1 'UNU-WIDER Government Revenue Dataset', 2020,
    www.wider.unu.edu/project/government-revenue-dataset.

in financing development, before Chapter 2 goes on to summarise tax revenue performance across African countries. Chapter 3 explores how revenue mobilisation from firms can be improved, with Chapter 4 expanding the discussion to personal income taxation. Chapter 5 then broadens the analysis to encompass how tax and expenditure systems can contribute to achieving equity and an enhanced state building process. Finally, Chapter 6 summarises the lessons learnt and how the development challenges faced by African countries may best be addressed in terms of improved revenue mobilisation.

The 'Park' market located in Jos, Nigeria.
Photo: Andrew Moore.

"A redistributive state needs resources and a strategy to mobilise significant amounts of revenue, and must focus on broad-based taxes, such as income taxes and value added tax (VAT)."
Chapter 1, page 23

1. Financing for Development

The issue of how to finance an inclusive development agenda has long been a key concern, with, over the past decade, increased emphasis placed on mobilising domestic resources. A government can tap several sources in this regard. Some countries are blessed with an abundance of natural resources, meaning resource rents form a significant share of total government revenue.[2] Meanwhile, in many countries, foreign aid has – to varying degrees – been used to augment public spending. Additionally, governments can finance long-term public investment by issuing bonds (debt financing), selling them either on the domestic or global bond markets. Finally, tax collection capabilities enable governments to raise money that can then be used to deliver public goods and redistribute resources.

A diversified revenue base is important for a number of reasons. Due to their scale, financing for large infrastructure investments is limited in terms of how much can be raised through taxation and domestic borrowing. To overcome this, a substantial proportion of financing must come from external sources. Such borrowing should be within sustainable debt limits, with borrowing from the African Development Bank, World Bank and International Monetary Fund (IMF) of particular importance in countries that have limited access to financial markets. Moreover, bilateral aid can play an important catalytic role in easing access to external finance.

Borrowing, however, has its limits and carries risks, making the diversification of revenue sources all the more important. Given resource rents from finite natural resources shrink over time, African countries reliant on such rents can address this by investing in human capital and other activities capable of generating future income. Here, it should be noted that some natural resources (e.g. oil, gas, coal) carry the risk of being exhausted sooner than anticipated. Alternatively, governments can access revenue generated by tax-

---

2   Resource rents capture the lifetime value of an exploited resource net of production costs, including the normal return to the investor. Resource rents that accrue to the government equal the difference between the world market price and production costs, including the return to the firm that exploits the resource.

ing their countries' populations. Again, though, there are limits, as taxation carries economic costs.

Total government revenue comprises four components: 1) tax revenue; 2) non-tax revenue; 3) grants;[3] and 4) social security contributions (SSCs). African countries vary significantly in the degree to which they draw on these four revenue sources. In some countries (e.g. Angola, Botswana, Chad, Equatorial Guinea, Gabon, Mauritania, Nigeria, Republic of the Congo, South Sudan) non-tax revenue (resource rents) forms a significant share of revenues. SSCs, meanwhile, are insignificant in most countries, and, where they do exist, are relatively small (e.g. Angola, Cameroon, Mauritius, Rwanda, South Africa). Grants (aid) also vary across countries, though, with a few exceptions (e.g. Liberia, Lesotho, Sao Tome and Principe), are not a major source of revenue. Thus, it is tax revenue that constitutes the most important source of revenue for the majority of African governments, despite tax revenue performance varying considerably between countries, ranging from a tax-to-GDP ratio of 10% to a ratio of 30%.

African countries are diverse in terms of their economic structure, as well as the political factors affecting them, whether this be quality of institutions or having a weak sense of national identity due to past policies and historical events. Some countries are experiencing internal conflict, while others are suffering long-term decline in terms of both economic performance and governance. Unsurprisingly, mobilising domestic resources becomes considerably more difficult under such circumstances. In countries that have suffered an extended period of reverse development, limited external financing options and a constrained tax system often stand in the way of restoring state legitimacy, as can be seen in the case of Zimbabwe (Box 1).

How can fiscal systems be reformed to support a transition towards a productive and redistributive state? Across the world, building trust in fiscal systems is important for state legitimacy, with trust in public institutions an outcome of citizens' broader perceptions of the fiscal system. Prichard et al. (2019) suggest four key components to a broader fiscal contract that citizens will be willing to participate in. First, tax systems must be fair in terms

---

3   Grants are transfers to the general government from other governments or international organisations.

of their design and administration.[4] Second, tax burdens must be distributed equitably, with everyone paying their share. Third, tax revenues must be translated into effective public goods and services provision. And, fourth, governments administering tax systems must be accountable to taxpayers.

A redistributive state needs resources and a strategy to mobilise significant amounts of revenue, and must focus on broad-based taxes, such as income taxes and value added tax (VAT).

Repressive governments, though, tend to avoid tax sources that require a high degree of voluntary cooperation (such as income taxes and VAT), and instead focus on trade taxes, excise duties and resource rents, if available. Here, the trend of excessively taxing social media (e.g. Rwanda, Tanzania, Uganda, Zambia, Zimbabwe) and the mobile industry offers a good example of both coercive government behaviour and the appetite for short-term revenue gains. Governments often argue that tax policy changes are required to increase much-needed revenue. Social media taxes are, however, unlikely to become a significant source of revenue – rather, they are more likely to distort the social contract between citizens and government, negatively impacting the willingness of the former to pay other taxes (e.g. income taxes).

The appetite for short-term revenue gains can also have detrimental effects on income generation and future tax revenue. In this context, a challenge for governments is how to move away from introducing a number of 'small' taxes towards a broad-based, less distortive taxation system, which is not only fair and capable of raising significant amounts of revenue, but can – combined with expenditures – be used for the purposes of redistribution. We will return to the question of whether tax systems in Africa are fair, as well as whether the fiscal system as a whole can redistribute. Before doing so, however, the next chapter summarises the revenue performance and characteristics of Africa's various tax regimes, illustrating how the structure of tax systems – and the potential therein for transforming them – varies in terms of current and future revenues.

---

4   In terms of what constitutes a fair tax system, tax theory centres on the horizontal and vertical equity theorem. Horizontal equity centres on equal treatment, with individuals at similar income and asset levels paying the same amount in taxes. Vertical equity, however, acknowledges that people with a greater ability to pay taxes should pay more. In practice, ability is approximated by income or wealth, with a tax considered progressive when richer households pay a higher share of their income.

Box 1. The challenges facing tax reform in Zimbabwe

Zimbabwe's recent development record disappointing, with GDP per capita falling close to 30% between 2000 and 2014. Moreover, the country's position relative to other African states has deteriorated across most social and infrastructure-related (e.g. access to water, sanitation, electricity) indicators. The overall situation is further constrained due to traditional sources of public finance – such as donor funding, and domestic and foreign borrowing – having dried up. This lack of finance has put pressure on national budgets, resulting in the government issuing treasury bills and borrowing heavily from the central bank. The consequence of this is a vicious cycle that is now difficult to break.

Addressing Zimbabwe's economic situation is a challenging task. The country must identify a long-term path towards faster growth in GDP, employment and incomes, accompanied by rapid progress on poverty reduction and other elements of the global sustainable development agenda. Doing so will require overcoming major structural challenges, including a large infrastructure gap, an inefficient government and an unfriendly business climate. Restarting the Zimbabwean economy thus involves a combination of difficult policy options. While financing investment through taxation may have a negative impact on household welfare in the immediate term, benefits can accrue over the long term. If the institutional environment is supportive and a reasonable return can be generated, investments may be self-financing. However, where investments have a low return, the combined impact of taxation and infrastructure investment will lower household welfare (Lofgren and Cicowiez, 2018).

The decline in GDP and the taxable base, as well as the increasing informalisation of economic activity, have constrained the tax system's effectiveness when it comes to raising an adequate level of government revenue (Masiyandima and Mlambo, 2018). In particular, the informalisation of the Zimbabwean economy has challenged the revenue authority's work by drastically changing the structure and composition of industry from large and easy-to-tax corporations employing many workers, to micro-, small- and medium-sized difficult-to-tax enterprises, each with only a small number of workers. Within a challenging institutional environment, the government faces a difficult task taxing itself out of a macroeconomic crisis. Rebuilding the social contract requires reform of the tax system, and that the government demonstrates competence and fairness in its public spending. Similarly, obtaining access to external finance requires the government to not only move forward on public service delivery, but commit to governance reforms.

Containers sit on a ship waiting to be offloaded at Mogadishu's port in Somalia. Photo: AMISOM/Tobin Jones.

"Trade taxes remain an important source of revenue in many African countries, with trade tax revenue as a share of total tax revenue rising above 40% in some cases."

Chapter 2, page 24

2. How Much Tax Revenue Do Countries Collect?

Tax revenue performance is often measured as a share of gross domestic product (GDP), with revenue performance tending to increase when GDP per capita increases (Figure 1). However, the amount a state taxes its citizens differs considerably from country to country. For example, among rich countries, some (e.g. Ireland, New Zealand, Sweden) levy close to 35% of GDP, while others (e.g. Germany, the Netherlands) levy 25%. A few rich countries (e.g. Saudi Arabia, Kuwait) levy hardly any taxes at all.

1. Tax revenue performance of all countries by income group (2017)

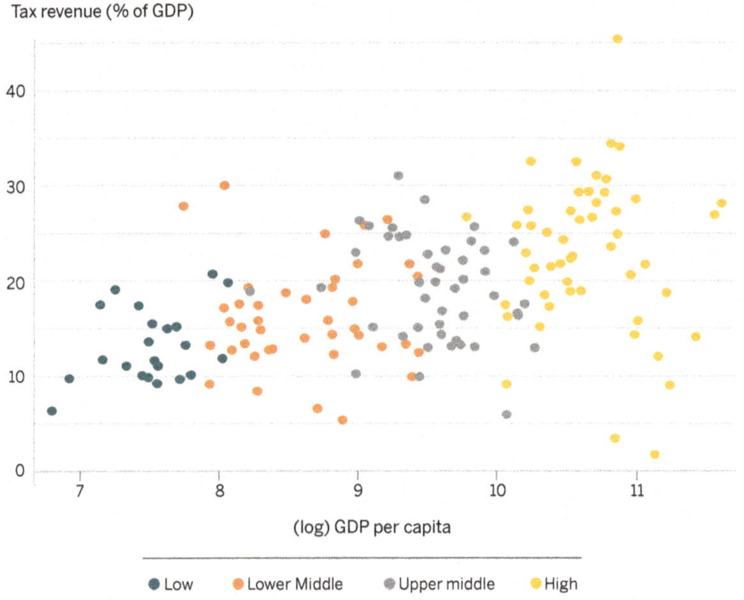

Source: UNU-WIDER Government Revenue Dataset (GRD)

Tax revenue performance across Africa varies greatly (Figure 2).[5,6] On the one hand, four African countries (Lesotho, Namibia, Seychelles, South Africa) feature among the top 15 countries globally; on the other hand, seven of the bottom 15 countries are from the region (Comoros, Democratic Republic of the Congo, Equatorial Guinea, Guinea-Bissau, Madagascar, Somalia, Sudan). Moreover, the tax capacity of a significant number of the region's countries falls below 15% of GDP, which is viewed as the minimum level if a state is to become viable and ensure sustainable growth (Gaspar et al., 2016).

Some observers object to tax performance being measured using a highly uncertain indicator such as GDP, which excludes certain activities and so is often underestimated, particularly in economies with large agricultural and

2. Tax revenue performance of African countries (2017)

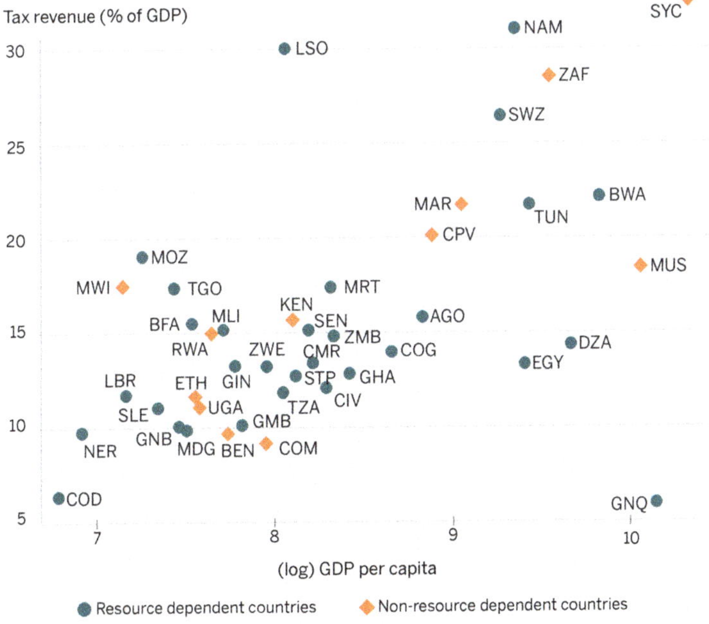

informal sectors. Regarding tax performance, the underestimation of GDP implies that tax performance (tax-to-GDP ratio) is worse than current estimates suggest. In Tanzania, for example, where overall revenue performance was 12% of GDP in 2013–2014, factoring in the informal economy suggests the real tax yield is closer to 6% of GDP (World Bank, 2015).

An alternative measure involves looking at tax revenue performance in per capita terms: the absolute amount of tax revenue divided by population size. Here again, the amount of revenue mobilised varies enormously. In the Democratic Republic of the Congo, for example, per capita revenue is USD 66, meaning that redistributing all tax revenues would gives each citizen 17 US cents per day. A number of countries collect less than USD 500 per capita (the countries between the Democratic Republic of the Congo and Cameroon in Figure 3), while at the next level up several countries raise revenue in the range of USD 500–1,000 per capita (Kenya–Lesotho). Finally, there are a number of countries that raise more than USD 1,000 per capita (Angola–Seychelles). The fact that revenues are apparently so low can partially be attributed to the data not capturing all tax payments.

The data presented in this report are tax revenues collected by central governments, as cross-country data for local government taxes in Africa are unavailable. In most African countries, though, central government revenues far outstrip local revenue sources – in Tanzania, for example, locally raised revenue accounts for approximately 10% of total local government revenue, with the remaining 90% consisting of intergovernmental transfers funded by revenue collected at a central government level.[7] This does not, however, imply that local government or municipal taxes are unimportant from a tax policy perspective (see Chapter 5).

---

5   A related measure of tax performance is the concept of tax effort analysis, which controls for various structural factors, such as colonial legacy, economic structure and state capacity. During the period 1984–2004, average tax performance in sub-Saharan Africa was – given the structural characteristics of African economies – in line with what might be expected (Mkandawire, 2010), with a more recent study going as far as saying that sub-Saharan Africa actually performed better than other regions in the world (Yohou and Goujon, 2017). The implication of this is that tax revenue performance is not only dependent on tax system efficiency, but on underlying structural characteristics.

6   Most figures use ISO country codes, which are explained in Appendix 1.

3. Per capita tax revenues (average 2015–2018)

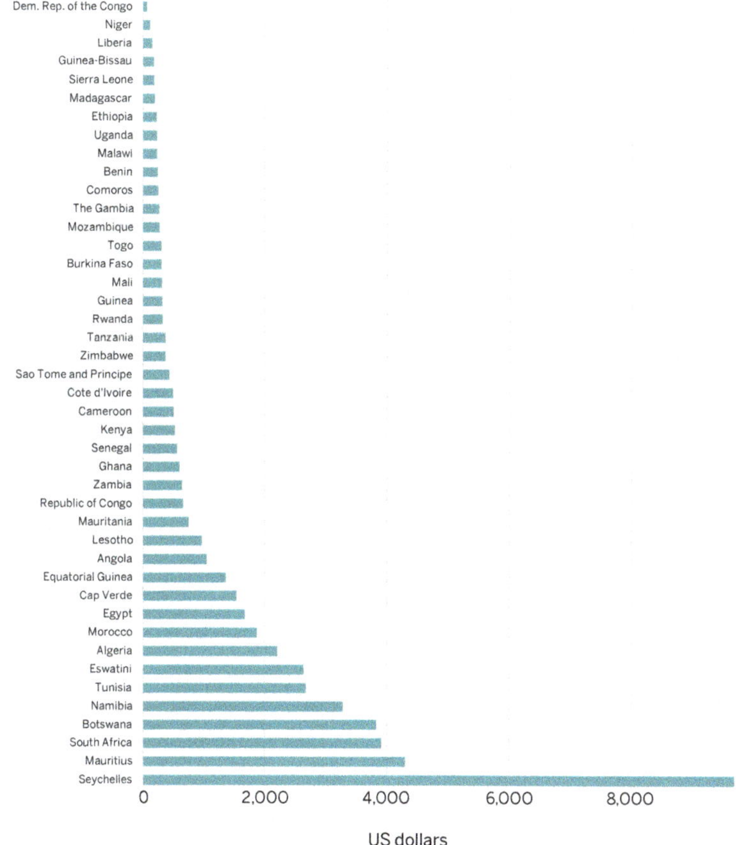

Source: Own calculations based on GRD

---

7   Fjeldstad et al. (2014) summarise some additional findings on the importance of central government revenue. In Botswana, rural councils and urban areas receive, respectively, 92% and 62% of their total revenues from central government. In Uganda, 88% of local government revenue consists of transfers from central government, while in Nigeria, local councils receive, on average, 78% of their revenue from transfers. In Liberia, meanwhile, local councils receive all their revenue from central government transfers. South Africa is the exception, with local governments generating the bulk of their revenues (89% in 2007) from their 'own' sources.

Regardless, even in countries with highly centralised systems, a relatively good tax revenue performance in the range of 20% translates to very low per capita revenue. Mozambique, for instance, has a tax-to-GDP ratio of close to 20%, which in per capita terms equates to approximately USD 270, around 70 times less than the top-ten average for rich countries (USD 19,000). Even if the country's tax performance were to be doubled to 40% of GDP (which is unrealistic), thereby doubling the per capita revenue to USD 540, this still only gives each citizen USD 1.5 per day. Thus, in order to increase tax revenue significantly, it is necessary to both enlarge the tax base and to develop ways of taxing it.

Table 1 illustrates the importance of improving tax systems while achieving high, sustained economic growth, as applied to Kenya.[8] In 2016, Kenya's tax-to-GDP ratio was 16%, which equates to a per capita tax revenue of USD 516. In a scenario involving high economic growth (7%) and improved tax performance (30% of GDP), tax per capita can increase by 262% over a 15-year period (2015–2030). However, the same improvement in tax performance coupled with a growth performance of 3% means that tax revenue per capita only increases by 88%; or, with a growth performance of 1%, by a mere 40%. The intermediate case, with a tax-to-GDP ratio of 23% – which is perhaps slightly more realistic in terms of revenue performance – shows an increase in per capita revenue of close to 150% in the high-growth (7%) scenario, and of 40% in the 3% growth scenario. While we do not focus directly on economic growth in this report, the unavoidable challenge arising from these figures is that tax revenue performance needs to be increased alongside high, inclusive growth. Alternately, in the language of taxation, a significant improvement in revenue mobilisation requires both that the tax base (GDP) is growing, and that the revenue authority has the capacity to exploit this growing tax base.

---

8   The starting year is based on average numbers for 2015–2017. The initial situation is a tax-to-GDP ratio of 16% and a tax per capita of USD 516 (PPP). In all scenarios, population growth of 3% is assumed.

Table 1:

Alternative scenarios of economic growth, tax-to-GDP ratio and tax revenue per capita

Economic Growth (%)	Tax-to-GDP ratio (%)	Tax per capita 2030 (USD)
7	16	915
3	16	516
1	16	385
7	23	1.315
3	23	743
1	23	553
7	30	1.715
3	30	969
1	30	722

Source: Own calculations

Composition of tax revenue[9]

What a particular country taxes varies widely. Direct taxes generally represent large tax bases, with the income tax component becoming more important as total revenue increases. Among rich, high-tax countries, direct taxes contribute more than half of total tax revenue, while among African countries a more diversified pattern emerges (Figure 4). In some (e.g. Kenya,

---

9   In this report we distinguish between direct and indirect taxes. Direct taxes are taxes levied on incomes, profits and property, while indirect taxes are levied on consumption of goods and services. Direct taxes distinguish between individuals and firms, and sources of income (capital and labour). Indirect taxes include various tax instruments, such as VAT/sales taxes, import duties, export taxes and excise duties.

Malawi, Mozambique) direct taxes contribute half of all tax revenue, rising to close to 60% in South Africa. It is also worth noting that in some countries with low tax-to-GDP ratios, direct taxes contribute close to 40% of total revenue. Additionally, countries differ in the composition of their direct taxes (see Chapter 3).

4. Contribution of direct taxes to total tax revenue (average 2015–2018)

Direct tax revenue (% of total tax revenue)

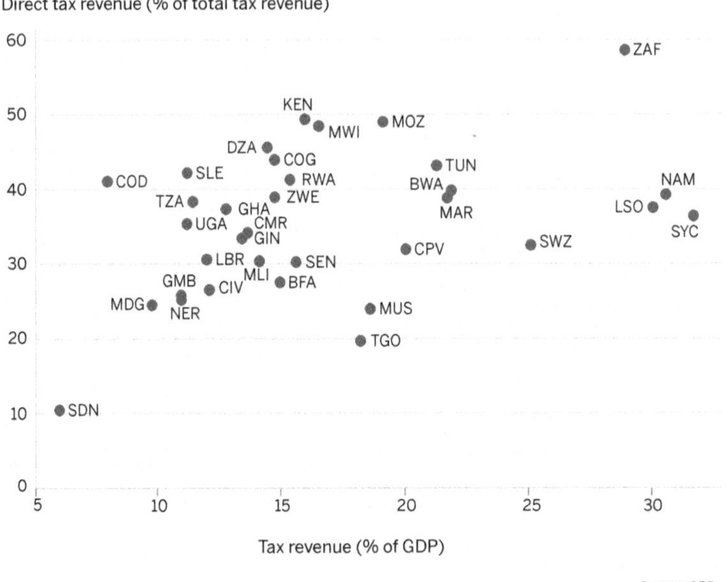

Tax revenue (% of GDP)

Source: GRD

Indirect taxes – which can be divided into trade taxes, VATs and excise duties – remain the most important revenue source in many African countries.[10] VATs in particular have become an important revenue source in a number of countries, contributing 30–40% of total revenue (Figure 5). Excise duties on petroleum products, as well as on alcohol, tobacco and beverages (sin-prod-

---

10 As income and indirect taxes together constitute total tax revenue, in Figure 4 the indirect tax revenue contribution equates to the remaining percentage needed to give a sum of 100% once direct tax revenue is factored in.

ucts), constitute another important indirect tax when it comes to domestic resource mobilisation (Figure 6). Moreover, excise duties targeting CO2 emissions represent an unexploited tax in most African countries (except South Africa), and have considerable revenue potential.

A recent trend across African countries has been to increase excise duties on the internet and mobile industry, resulting in the sector becoming excessively taxed.[11] For example, recent tax hikes on internet services, mobile phones (air-time) and mobile financial transactions in Kenya have seemingly increased tax evasion and substitution, while negatively affecting the wider economy (Ndung'u, 2019). The benefits of low-cost mobile banking technology – which have improved access to financial services, particularly in ru-

5. Contribution of VAT to total tax revenue (average 2015–2018)

Source: GRD

---

11 Approximately 26% of taxes and fees paid by the mobile industry in 12 sub-Saharan African countries (Cameroon, Chad, Democratic Republic of the Congo, Ghana, Guinea, Madagascar, Niger, Rwanda, Senegal, Sierra Leone, South Africa, Tanzania) were sector-specific taxes (Rogers and Pedros, 2017).

ral areas – have been significant, and include: increased productivity among small farmers; reduced poverty; and, for poor households, greater food security and opportunities for self-employment.[12] Notably, these impacts have been more pronounced for female-headed households. Excessive taxation, however, threatens to reverse such progress.

Trade taxes remain an important source of revenue in many African countries (Figure 7), with trade tax revenue as a share of total tax revenue rising above 40% in some cases (Somalia being the extreme example, at 80%). Below this level, a large number of countries have a trade taxes revenue share of approximately 15–20%. Thus, despite the average tariff rate on imports from intra-African trade being lower than imports from the rest of the world, the move towards an Africa Continental Free Trade Area is likely to affect total tax revenue.[13] If the fall in trade taxes is not compensated for by an in-

6. Contribution of excise duties to total tax revenue (average 2015–2018)

Excise duties (% of total tax revenue)

Tax revenue (% of GDP)

Source: GRD

---

12   Suri and Jack (2016) show that access to the M-Pesa technological platform increased per capita consumption levels and lifted 194,000 Kenyan households (2% of households) out of poverty.

crease in other taxes, especially VATs, then the short-to-medium-term effects of trade reform are likely to result in revenue losses, with previous studies having shown that countries with weak fiscal capacity are more likely to have difficulties compensating for such losses. In addition, many resource-dependent countries already have very low tax revenues, which further complicates any process of fast recovery from revenue losses.

7. Contribution of trade tax revenue to total tax revenue (average 2015–2018)

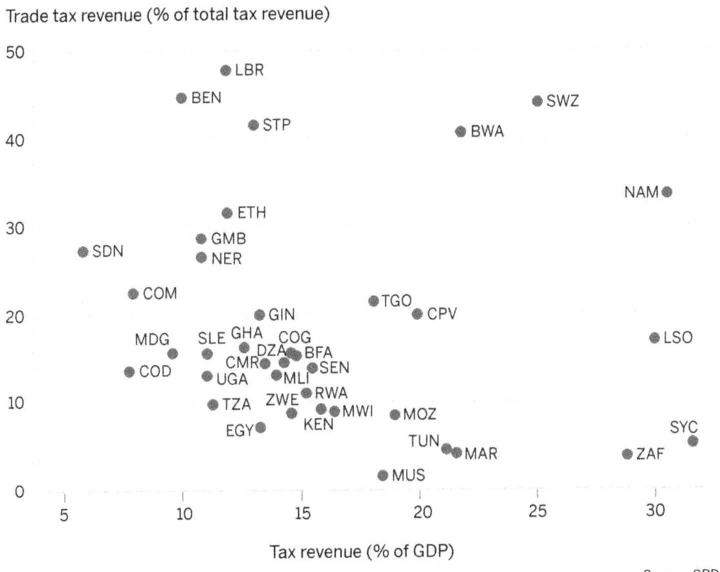

13 For example, there are concerns that the Africa Continental Free Trade Area will have a negative short-term impact on tax revenues. Tariff revenues would decline by less than 1.5% for most countries, except for the Democratic Republic of the Congo (3.4%), the Gambia (2.7%), the Republic of the Congo (2.1%), and Zambia (1.6%) (World Bank, 2020).

Tax reform and changes in tax revenue

Stepping back from the current tax revenue structures of African countries highlighted above, a related question is how tax revenues and taxation structures have changed over time. Since the mid-1990s, a number of African countries have seen significant improvements in revenue performance. Figure 8 shows the average tax-to-GDP ratio for 2016–2018 on the vertical axis, and the average tax-to-GDP ratio for the mid-1990s on the horizontal axis, with countries above the 45-degree line having improved their performance since the latter period. Within the group of countries that in the mid-1990s had a revenue performance of around 10% of GDP, several (Burkina Faso, Malawi, Mozambique, Rwanda, Senegal, Togo) have increased their tax-to-GDP ratios significantly. There has also been progress in countries that had higher mid-1990s tax-to-GDP ratios, while the countries that have not seen any improve-

8. Changes in tax revenue performance

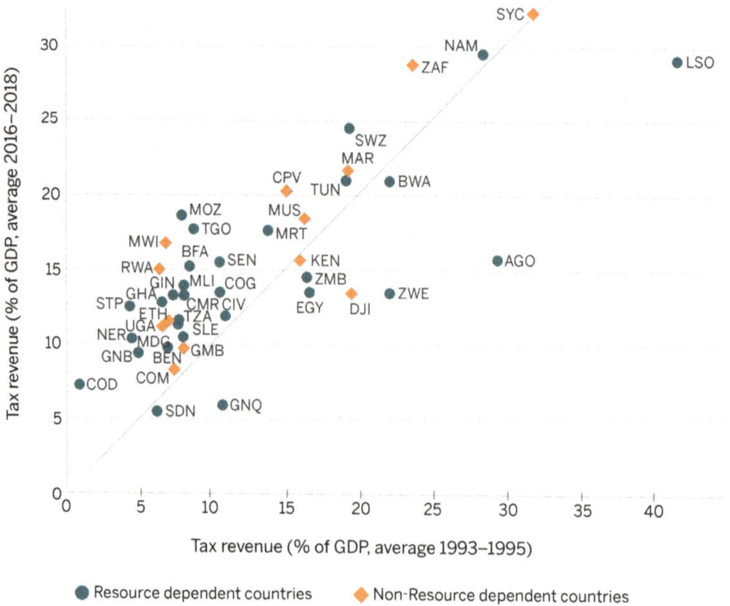

ments are, to a large degree, resource dependent. With regard to tax structures, earlier periods (1980–2005) saw an upward trend in indirect taxes, with revenue from income taxes remaining almost constant (Keen and Mansour, 2009). More recent data suggest that income taxes have increased in importance relative to indirect taxes (Figure 9).

What, then, explains the progress outlined above? Many countries have enhanced tax collection through tax policy reforms, which typically include measures aimed at simplifying the tax system, reducing exemptions, and reforming indirect taxes on goods and services. Revenue authority reforms, meanwhile, generally involve managing compliance risks and investing in capacity to deal with large taxpayers. Akitoby et al. (2019), in analysing large tax revenue gains in Burkina Faso, the Gambia, Mauritania, Rwanda, Senegal and Uganda, find that successful tax reforms require political commitment

9. Changes in direct tax revenue performance

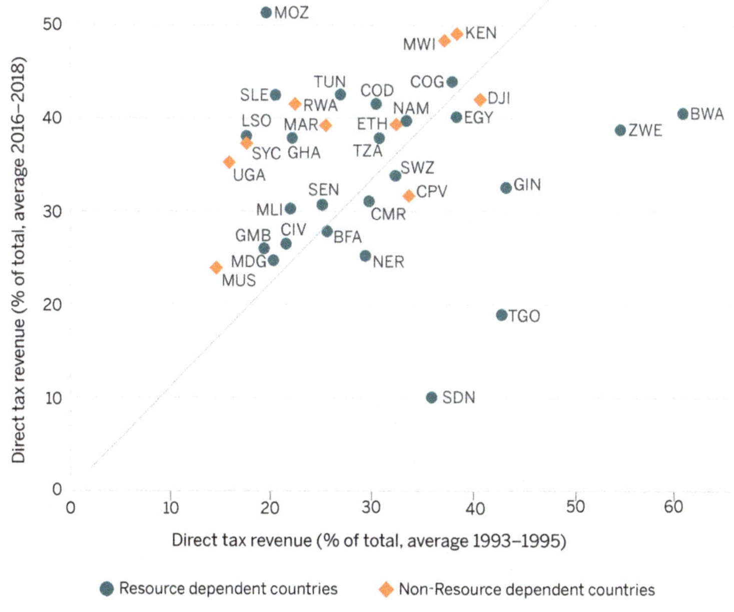

Source: GRD

and key stakeholder buy-in, and that countries undertaking both revenue administration and tax policy reforms tend to see larger and persistent gains. Ahlerup et al. (2015), meanwhile, show that reform of tax administrations is important when it comes to increasing revenue, particularly from income taxes.

Reforming tax systems is an ongoing task and, following two decades of relatively good economic performance, which in turn have generated higher incomes and increased wealth, opportunities are now available to exploit these revenue sources. There are significant contrasts in the composition of income tax revenue in rich, high-tax countries and African countries: in the former, income taxes are mainly the result of taxing individuals, while in the latter, income taxes are largely derived from taxing firms. The low share of corporate tax payments in rich, high-tax countries is partly a reflection of how their tax systems are designed. For example, tax systems in Nordic countries are dual income, which separates the taxation of labour from the taxation of capital income. The share of profits distributed as dividends to owners combined with other capital income are taxed individually at a flat rate, and combined with a progressive tax on wage income.[14] The remaining share of profits is taxed at the firm level.[15]

African revenue authorities, building on their recent drive to register taxpayers, must design a less complex, easier-to-administer income tax system, while reducing the costs of compliance. Here, it has been suggested that a dual-tax system has features that could be workable in African countries (Bird and Zolt, 2011). Moreover, financing for social protection programmes

---

14 In Sweden, for example, capital incomes are taxed at a rate of 30%, while wage income tax is 30%–35%, depending on location. Beyond a certain income threshold, an additional 20% tax is imposed on employment incomes earned above the threshold. Meanwhile, the tax on profits equals 21%.

15 An alternative comprehensive system is the flat-tax system, which has become popular in Eastern Europe. One important difference between a flat- and a dual-tax system is that the flat-tax system lacks the progressive labour income features found in a dual-tax system.

16 Such costs vary depending on the assumptions made about scale and coverage, with some estimates suggesting a range of 5–10% of GDP. The average tax-to-GDP ratio across sub-Saharan Africa is approximately 15%, and so increasing the budget by one-third to two-thirds represents a significant rise. Moreover, given many countries are already collecting revenue at a level considered in line with what can be expected, doing so would be a formidable challenge.

must be factored in if their sustainability is to be ensured – the costs of such programmes are significant, with donor funding likely to remain the major source of funding for a considerable length of time.[16] Given this, introducing fragmented tax policy changes, including earmarking specific indirect taxes (such as excise duties and VATs), is not a viable long-term strategy. Social security taxes should be integrated into the income tax system, with broad and uniform application of such taxes reducing the risk of further informalisation of African economies. In the following two chapters, we shed light on some of the key issues related to income taxes, both in terms of corporate taxation and individual income taxes.

Woman works in her cassava field in Mkuranga district, Tanzania.
Photo H. Holmes/RTB.

"A distinction must be made between agricultural sector agents operating on a purely subsistence level and those with operations closer to commercial activities."

Chapter 3, page 39

3. Taxing Firms

Despite the overwhelming proportion of informal production activities in Africa, the region's tax systems are more dependent on corporate tax revenue than others in the world. In Tanzania, for example, large enterprises (400 companies), primarily based in Dar es Salaam, contribute almost half the total value of tax revenues (World Bank, 2015). African countries have a similar corporate tax system to other world regions, and, as elsewhere, statutory profit tax rates differ. Corporate profit tax rates in Africa vary from a low of 15% (Mauritius) to a high of 35% (Chad, Democratic Republic of the Congo, Equatorial Guinea, Gabon, Guinea, Guinea-Bissau, Sudan, Zimbabwe), with the median rate being 30%. In many African countries, therefore, those firms that do pay taxes shoulder a high tax burden.

The amount a firm pays in profit tax depends on gross profit adjusted for a range of legal deductions, exemptions and sector-specific tax incentives, combined with other taxes on production. Targeted exemption schemes, which often have a geographical focus, are regularly in place to support specific sectors, such as agro-processing, mining and manufacturing. Thus, the amount firms actually pay – their effective tax burden – differs significantly from the statutory rates. In countries where the statutory profit tax rate is 25%, for example, the actual tax on profits varies from 18% to 60% (Figure 10).[17] In Zimbabwe, numerous exemptions decrease the statutory rate of 35% to a de facto rate of less than 20%. In other countries, however, the de facto profit rate is significantly higher than the statutory rate, often due to the same/similar taxes being enforced multiples times at different government administrative levels.

In addition to potentially very high tax rates, the tax system itself can be

---

17 Profit taxes as a percentage of profits measures the amount of taxes and mandatory contributions payable by businesses after accounting for deductions and exemptions, as a share of profits. Taxes withheld (such as personal income taxes) or collected and remitted to tax authorities (such as VATs and sales taxes) are excluded.

18 The time to prepare and pay taxes equates to the time, in hours per year, it takes to prepare, file and pay (or withhold) three major types of taxes: corporate income taxes; VATs or sales taxes; and labour taxes, including payroll taxes and social security contributions. The number of payments by businesses is the total number of taxes paid by businesses, including electronic filing, with the tax counted as paid once a year even if actual payments are made more frequently.

10. Statutory profit tax and *de facto* profit tax rates

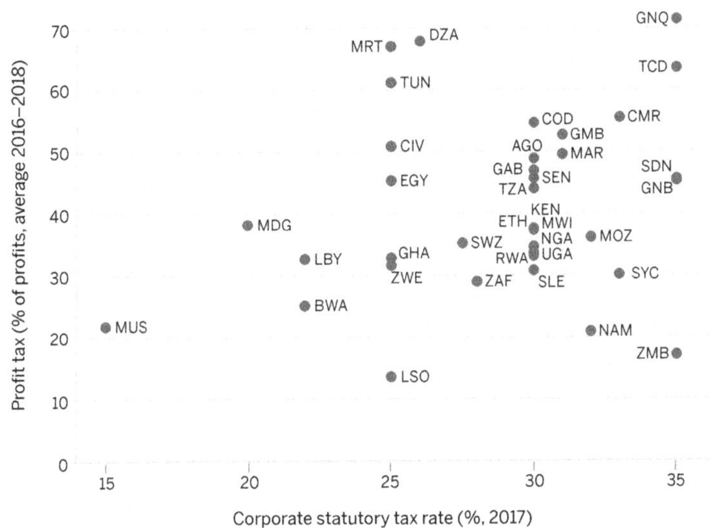

Source: GRD/World Development Indicators (WDI)

complex, as reflected in the number of taxes and the time needed to prepare and pay them.[18] In rich, high-tax countries – such as New Zealand, Norway and Sweden – the number of taxes paid by the corporate sector is around five. While in several African countries (e.g. Mauritius, Morocco, Rwanda, South Africa, Tunisia) the number of taxes paid is approximately ten, in others (e.g. Burkina Faso, Cameroon, Nigeria, Republic of Congo, Senegal, Tanzania, Togo, Zimbabwe) the number is 50 or more. Having a large number of taxes increases compliance costs, which in turn incentivises tax avoidance.

A tax system's complexities affects distribution of the tax burden between firms. In Ethiopia, for example, approximately 42% of corporate tax declarations yield no taxable income and no tax revenue. Among those firms that do pay, small firms face the highest (effective) tax burden, middle-sized firms the lowest, with large-sized firms somewhere in between. Mascagni and Mengistu (2016) argue that small firms do not have the capacity or resources to fully exploit the tax system, as doing so adds to costs in terms of hiring the necessary expertise to advise on legal deductions. On the other hand, though large firms have the expertise to minimise taxes, they are highly visible to tax authorities, and therefore face limits on the extent to which they can apply aggressive tax-minimising strategies.

In South Africa, the effective tax rate is, across all sectors, far lower than the statutory corporate income tax rate, which points to how exemptions, allowances and other legal deductions reduce companies' tax burdens. As in Ethiopia, small companies bear the highest tax burden, with large-sized companies paying slightly more than medium-sized companies, which have the lowest tax burden (Carreras et al., 2017).

Small- and medium-sized enterprises must often self-assess their taxable income. In a context of imperfect enforcement mechanisms, the incentives to deliberately underreport income and profits are considerable. A number of factors can, though, improve the situation. These include new technology, such as electronic filing systems, which can reduce a firm's compliance costs and therefore improve tax compliance. In South Africa, for example, e-filing was made compulsory, with paper submissions no longer accepted. In Uganda, a combination of taxpayer registration campaigns and a new electronic filing system increased the number of taxpayers filing returns (Jouste et al., 2019). In Nigeria, characteristics that influence a firm's willingness to adopt new systems include the business owner's level of education, whether they received training, and their trust in the tax administration (Efobi et al., 2019). At a broader level, compliance is also associated with how a firm perceives the risk of detection or having a penalty imposed, as well as its perception of whether other businesses are complying and its satisfaction with public services.[19] While merely fixing one of the several factors impacting compliance may not always yield long-lasting results, it nevertheless – combined with overall tax administration improvements, enhanced perceptions of corruption, and simplifications of the tax system – increases the likelihood that compliance will improve.[20]

In sum, taxing the corporate sector should be fair, with the underlying

---

19 Fjeldstad et al. (2020) find this to be the case in terms of the electronic filing of VAT transactions in Tanzania. A study on Ethiopia, meanwhile, suggests coercive and persuasive messaging concerning a forthcoming audit significantly reduces tax evasion in the short term. Moreover, the effects tend to be higher in businesses commonly suspected of high tax-evasion rates (Shimeles et al., 2017).

choice not based on whether a tax is progressive in nature (as may be the case in the taxing of an individual's income). Neither is it optimal to place a greater tax burden on sectors that are more productive and therefore likely to be future employers. In a fair tax system, effective tax rates should be similar – or, at least, not deviate too greatly – between firms. In practise, however, there are several challenges to achieving this.

Large taxpayers and illicit flows

Even if the tax burden of large firms is relatively lower than that of small corporations, the mere size of the former's operations implies that a significant share of corporate revenue comes from the largest decile. In both South Africa and Ethiopia, the largest 10% of firms contribute close to 90% of corporate revenue. In South Africa, it is also among the largest 10% that tax authorities are most likely to find firms engaging in profit shifting. While this does not necessarily involve a large number of firms, the sheer size of those that do engage in profit shifting implies that revenue losses may be considerable in some cases.

Estimating revenue losses due to cross-border financial flows is inherently difficult as such information is not revealed directly. Indirect approaches have been used in the literature, with the estimates in Figure 11 a recalculation of results presented in Cobham and Jansky (2018).[21] While these estimates should be interpreted with caution, it can be seen that revenue losses vary between countries and can be quite significant. In around half the sample, revenue losses are in the range of 15–25% of total tax revenue, which in countries with a revenue-to-GDP ratio of 15%, amounts to revenue losses in the range of 2–4% of GDP. Though this represents a valuable portion of revenue performance, it is not sufficient to dramatically change a country's fiscal position. Revenue losses of approximately 2–4% of GDP also equates to what governments forego due to exemption schemes in VATs, meaning that closing

---

20 Chuku et al. (2019) find empirical support for this situation in a number of African countries (Democratic Republic of the Congo, Egypt, Kenya, Nigeria, Zimbabwe).

21 Instead of presenting revenue losses as a share of GDP, we recalculated the loss in relation to total tax revenue.

11. Tax revenue losses (2013)

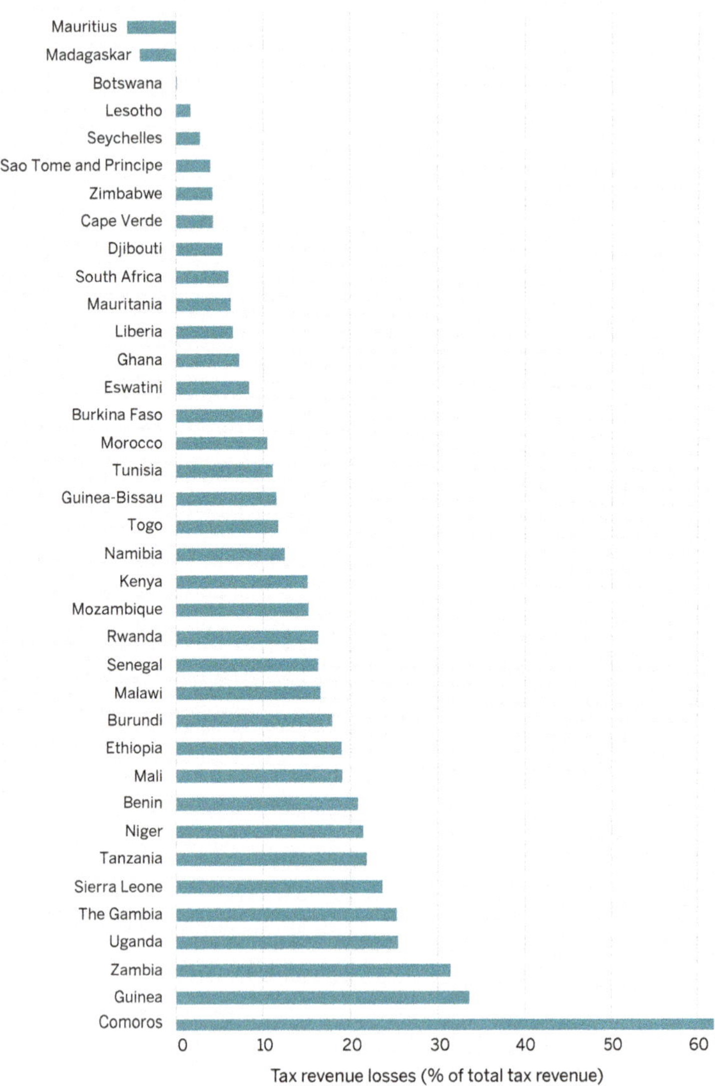

Source: Own calculations, based on Cobham and Jansky (2018)

both illicit flows and VAT gaps would add revenue in the range of 4–8% of GDP. In the Kenyan case discussed earlier (Table 1), closing both gaps would increase per capita tax from USD 516 (PPP) to USD 743 (PPP) – again, not a dramatic change, but still an important one.

How, then, can tax authorities improve compliance in large, complex sectors, and among large-scale taxpayers? Löffler et al. (2018) review practises for strengthening mining-sector taxation in four West African countries (Côte d'Ivoire, Guinea, Liberia, Sierra Leone). In their framework, they outline broad thematic themes that can assist governments in reducing tax evasion within the extractive industries, with, for example, the exploitation of third-party data increasingly important for revenue authorities around the world. In Liberia, access to detailed metal price data has been helpful to tax authorities conducting audits of the revenues and royalty payments reported by mining companies. As a consequence, significant adjustments have been made to reported income (especially in cases of related-party sales), and in turn the amount of tax payable. Moreover, participating in global networks, such as Base Erosion Profit Shifting (BEPS) and the Convention on Mutual Administrative Assistance in Tax Matters (MAC), supports government-to-government information exchange, which is important for strengthening international tax auditing.

Collaboration and information exchanges between different government entities is also important. With regard to mining taxation, tax and customs administrations, as well as mining authorities, can benefit greatly from collaboration on sector-specific issues. In Liberia, for example, a mining revenue taskforce was established to facilitate information sharing across agencies and tackle issues of mutual concern. The taskforce noted that the government was not engaged in sampling or testing minerals prior to their being exported by the mining companies, who instead engaged the services of independent inspection companies. As a result, royalties were being determined by the mining companies through a self-assessment system, without any mechanism for the Liberian revenue authority to validate them. The taskforce therefore developed new procedures that allowed for random mineral sampling/testing by the government.

Strengthening analytical modelling capacity within governments and revenue authorities is important for reforming tax policy. Findings from a financial modelling exercise in Côte d'Ivoire, for example, indicated significant tax losses arising from tax holidays, which prompted the government to remove several previously permitted tax exemptions. In addition, taxation can be enforced digitally by exploiting data a government already possesses. Using customs data, for example, it may be possible to estimate revenue losses arising from transfer mispricing, which multinational firms in South Africa engage in in order to shift taxable profits to low-tax countries. Even where the estimated tax losses are negligible as a share of corporate taxes paid, the costs of addressing these anomalies is very low compared to the gains (Wier, 2020).

Corporate taxation, informality and fairness

Taxation within Africa's corporate sector is generally unfair, which undermines trust and the willingness to pay taxes. This is due, firstly, to firms registered as taxpayers experiencing unequal effective tax burdens; and, secondly, the formal/informal divide. A situation in which some firms are taxed only partially, if at all, and some are fully captured in the tax net also has broader implications for economic growth and employment generation. Unfair competition from informal production activities is one of the major obstacles reported by African firms wishing to expand production. Labour productivity (and wages) is, on average, much lower in informal firms than formal firms. Thus, excessive taxation of highly productive firms may slow economic and social progress – especially in terms of capital accumulation and productivity growth. This in turn impacts future income opportunities.

Informality is conceptualised in many ways in the literature. Here, we define formality as those activities within the purview of state laws and regulations, and informality as those activities that lie outside these boundaries (Kanbur, 2017). From a taxation perspective, informality consists of economic activities that are not registered by tax authorities, and includes the productive activities of both those with very small and very high incomes.[22] In a fair tax system, a distinction must be made between activities that may or may not be taxed. Within informal firms, for example, a distinction can be made between, on the one hand, subsistence enterprises and micro enterpris-

---

22 Formality and informality are not clearly distinguished, as many informal employees still require a local business licence. As digitalisation increases, it would not be too difficult to condition the issuing of a licence on being registered as a taxpayer, either as an individual or as a company.

es, and, on the other hand, small- and medium-sized businesses, with the latter considered liable for taxes (Joshi et al., 2014). Similarly, a distinction must be made between agricultural sector agents operating on a purely subsistence level and those with operations closer to commercial activities. Subsistence activities often result in earnings below what might be considered the minimum tax threshold, meaning that in such cases efficiency and equity losses are likely to outweigh broader governance gains.

Tax systems across Africa have, for a long time, distinguished between small, medium and large firms, with presumptive tax regimes introduced in many African countries aimed at reducing the administrative and compliance costs of smaller firms. Tax liabilities among these smaller firms are based on indirect measures, such as turnover, indicators (e.g. number of employees, floor space) or fixed lump-sum taxes. Over time, the presumptive taxpayers – whose tax burdens are usually low and fixed over long periods – are expected to mature into a regular tax regime of bookkeeping and returns filing. In reality, once a firm enters a presumptive regime, it is unlikely to migrate to the regular system (Bird and Zolt, 2011), due in part to the relatively low tax rate it enjoys compared to the equivalent rate in the latter system.

Moving towards a dual-income tax system offers a means of improving the coordination of existing presumptive tax regimes, and, over time, encouraging businesses to move to the regular tax system. In addition, it can help bring together the fragmented income tax systems that now exist in many African countries. Even so, given that African countries differ widely in terms of revenue performance and fiscal capacity, how and when a particular state moves towards a comprehensive system will likely vary.

Nevertheless, the underlying principle in all cases is to design a tax system that is fair and easy to understand. Tax systems that are complicated or time-consuming carry a high tax burden and are often enforced by weak institutions – combined with a general lack of trust, this contributes to an environment in which incentives to avoid paying taxes are accentuated.

Some of the many small garden plots in Bamako, Mali. Almost every piece of land is cultivated by small farmers who grow everything from lettuce to corn. Photo: Mark Fischer.

"A zero tolerance approach
to corruption is key to gaining
public support for land and
property taxation, and therefore legitimacy."

Chapter 4, page 49

4. Taxing Individuals

While personal income taxation (PIT) performance varies between African countries, closer inspection reveals a familiar pattern, with individual income taxes increasingly important as total revenue increases (Figure 12).

In terms of increasing revenue from individuals, revenue authorities face two problems. The first of these is that few individuals are registered with the tax authorities. In Uganda in 2013, approximately 200,000 individuals – a mere 2% of the labour force – were registered as individual taxpayers, with close to 70% of these being employees. In Kenya, 3.2 million of the country's near 49 million citizens filed income tax returns in 2018, a figure that, despite significant improvements over the years, still represents approximately only 10% of the labour force. Nevertheless, tax authorities have to start some-

12. Individual income taxes (average 2015–2018)

Individual tax (% of GDP)

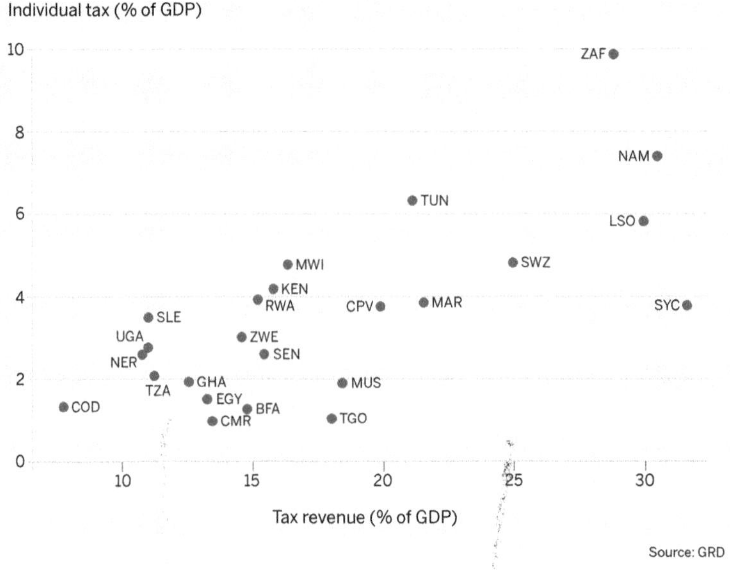

Source: GRD

where, meaning that citizens must first be identified and registered as taxpayers. Such registration should be part of a broader strategy involving individuals becoming beneficiaries of a social security system.

A second problem is that, even if taxpayers register, this does not necessarily translate into payment of taxes. A variety of factors explain individual compliance attitudes, though these tend to differ between countries. In a study based on four African countries (Kenya, South Africa, Tanzania, Uganda), individuals in South Africa and Kenya were found to be more likely to express a willingness to pay taxes if they perceived that enforcement made evasion more difficult (Ali et al., 2013). Moreover, empirical support was found in all four countries for the idea that individuals who are more satisfied with public service provision are more likely to have a tax-compliant attitude. However, the nature of this link differed between countries: in Kenya, respondents cited access to infrastructure such as roads and electricity as encouraging a tax-compliant attitude; in Tanzania and Uganda, respondents referred to education and health services; while in South Africa, respondents highlighted police services and the issuance of identity cards. In addition, knowledge and awareness of the tax system were shown to be important in South Africa and Tanzania, with those individuals who have difficulties in determining what taxes they are required to pay less likely to have a tax-compliant attitude than those who perceive the process as being relatively easy.

Developing a broader social contract also implies that PIT must be fair in terms of design and administration, and that tax burdens be equitably distributed. While PIT systems in African countries may be fair and progressive on paper, in reality this is almost certainly not the case. A major problem in analysing PIT in Africa is lack of data – only recently, and in only a few countries, have African tax authorities made registration data publicly available. Even then, obtaining a clear picture of whether income tax systems are progressive is difficult, as relatively few individuals are registered. A further complication is that tax duplication at both central and local government levels makes it difficult to evaluate who is paying taxes.

As well as broadening the PIT base, the tax system itself must be reformed and simplified. Though wage income taxes are often deducted at source for those employed in the private or public sectors, other non-wage incomes (allowances or income from other activities) are often not taxed at all. In

Uganda, for example, only one of the 71 top-ranking government officials has ever remitted an individual income tax other than that which is automatically withheld. Moreover, only a few companies associated with these individuals have remitted corporate taxes in the years under review (Kangave et al., 2016).

In general, company owners remit very low individual income taxes, as do many professionals (e.g. lawyers). This is sometimes due to a fragmented tax system making it difficult to differentiate between capital and wage incomes. For instance, self-employed owners can choose how much they wish to receive as a regular wage payment, versus how much profit they wish to distribute to themselves. If profits (or capital incomes) are taxed much lower than wages, owners or high-income, self-employed individuals are incentivised towards income-shifting practises. A dual-income tax system that imposes uniform tax rates on both wage and capital incomes can reduce these incentives.

Few wealthy individuals in the private or public sectors comply with their tax obligations, either not paying taxes at all or grossly under-declaring their income. As a consequence, very little tax is collected from this category of taxpayers. Any strategy for improving compliance among high-net-worth individuals (HNWIs) is likely to be more successful if tax rates are modest, as high rates may result in more tax evasion. Taxing HNWIs can be complicated from a political perspective, as economic elites often have strong political power, with strategies differing between countries. Generally, it is likely that multiple sources of information will be needed to triangulate identification of candidates whose incomes are not directly known.

Under-taxed HNWIs are a challenge not only in African countries but rich nations. In Scandinavian countries, for example, most of the population rarely if ever evade taxes, as their tax liability is transferred directly (by the employer) to the tax authorities. However, leaked data (the Panama papers and the Swiss leaks) combined with official documentation show pervasive tax evasion among the elite. The top 0.01% of Scandinavian wealth-holders, a group consisting of households holding more than $45 million in net wealth, evade 25%–30% of their personal taxes, which dwarfs the average evasion rate of approximately 3% (Alstadsæter et al., 2017).

A crucial issue in terms of obtaining the information necessary to tax

HNWIs is that they are not usually registered as taxpayers, and even if they are, it if often difficult to link taxable assets to the individual. The case of Uganda – which in 2015 established a HNWI unit within its already existing large-taxpayer unit, and has since been relatively successful in mobilising additional tax revenue – offers some important lessons on how to tax HNWIs (Waiswa et al., 2017). Taxing HNWIs involves politically well-connected individuals, and so care must be taken to treat all individuals equally. Having identified HNWIs, it is important to share information about taxpayers' rights and obligations, as this signals that all citizens – including politicians and the wealthy – are subject to auditing. More generally, the learning process should be acknowledged as continuous, requiring collaboration between various government departments and financial institutions. In the case of Uganda, and likely elsewhere in Africa, wealth is particularly concentrated in property and land ownership. Land transactions and significant rental incomes can be traced, as can large transactions in the financial markets (loans). Trade statistics, particularly large import and export bills, can also be traced to companies and individuals. Alternatively, at an individual level, those who are importing expensive cars or are shareholders in companies with large turnovers may be flagged as possible HNWIs.

While not all the necessary information may be available at once, it is important to make a start with whatever information is available, rather than waiting until comprehensive definitions and lists are available. In addition, it is possible to identify HNWIs in the first instance by combining various data sources with public knowledge (the rich are known), before a final selection is made based on certain criteria (income/wealth threshold). Collaboration between different departments is important, as is having a relatively independent revenue authority that can resist political pressure.

Taxing wealth

Taxing wealth – which comprises both financial and nonfinancial assets invested in residential buildings, as well as other nonfinancial assets such as land and businesses – is important in increasing how progressive a tax system is. However, determining a precise measure of how much wealth is available to tax is difficult in any economy. Recent data from the World Inequality Database suggest that some rich countries (e.g. Norway, Sweden, UK) have a wealth-to-GDP ratio of between 4 and 6, while the ratio in African countries varies between 1 and 3 (Table 2).[23] Based on this information, we can combine the wealth-to-GDP and tax-to-GDP ratios for a number of countries, and illustrate the potential revenue impact of a 1.4% wealth tax.[24]

The estimation assumes that a wealth tax does not currently exist, which, while clearly not the case in some rich countries, is more likely to be the situation in a number of African countries. Given that levels of wealth vary between countries, so the revenue impact will also vary. Among the selected African countries, additional revenue varies from 0.6% (Democratic Republic of the Congo, Lesotho) to 4.1% (Kenya). As the Kenyan example shows, adding taxes on illicit flows, wealth and VAT gaps will increase the Kenyan tax-to-GDP ratio from 16% to 27%, while reducing the tax gaps on income taxation is likely to bring the Kenyan tax-to-GDP ratio close to 30%. In sum, while a single tax-gap elimination cannot in itself dramatically change Kenya's (or an equivalent country's) fiscal position, efficient use of all available tax bases could shift revenue performance to close to 30% of GDP.

Difficulties arise when it comes to governments taxing financial assets, as such assets often cross borders. Moreover, the wisdom of taxing these financial assets may be questionable, as they represent an important source of investment finance. Many policymakers therefore agree on property taxes as a good solution. While the contribution of property taxes varies greatly between countries, figures for African countries – South Africa and Egypt excepted – remain very low, in most cases contributing to less than 1% of GDP. Property taxes have a number of advantages (Ali et al., 2017). First, they do not have a negative effect on production, while potentially encouraging more productive uses of land and property. Second, they are a progressive form of taxation, with a greater tax burden likely to be borne by households

---

23 Publications and data on wealth inequalities can be found at the World Inequalities Database (WID), https://wid.world/data/.

24 Estimating the value of wealth in any economy is complicated. Wealth is comprised of financial and non-financial assets invested in residential buildings, as well as other non-financial assets such as land and business assets. Approaches to taxing wealth differ. Financial wealth is taxed implicitly through capital gains taxes. A return on financial assets of 7% and a tax on capital gains of 20% equates to an annual tax of 1.4% on total wealth. An alternate approach is to move towards a death tax (or inheritance tax), whereby total wealth is taxed before relatives can claim their inheritance. The latter case requires legal authorities that can value the assets left behind.

Table 2: Wealth taxation

Country	Wealth-to-GDP ratio	Tax-to-GDP ratio (%)	Tax-to-GDP ratio +wealth tax (%)	% unit change
United Kingdom	6.4	26.5	35.4	8.9
Sweden	5.2	33.8	41.0	7.2
Norway	4.5	28.5	34.8	6.3
Kenya	2.9	15.8	19.9	4.1
Liberia	2.3	11.8	15.0	3.2
Comoros	1.8	7.9	10.5	2.6
South Africa	1.7	28.8	31.1	2.3
Ethiopia	1.6	11.8	14.1	2.3
Namibia	1.6	30.5	32.7	2.2
Morocco	1.5	21.5	23.6	2.1
Tunisia	1.3	21.1	22.9	1.8
Egypt	1.2	13.3	14.9	1.6
Dem. Rep. of the Congo	1.2	7.7	9.3	1.6
Senegal	1.1	15.4	17.0	1.6
Malawi	1.0	16.4	17.9	1.5
Madagascar	0.9	9.5	10.8	1.3
Guinea-Bissau	0.9	9.4	10.7	1.3
Gambia, The	0.9	10.8	12.0	1.2
Mali	0.9	13.9	15.1	1.2
Botswana	0.8	21.7	22.9	1.2
Zambia	0.8	14.5	15.7	1.2
Cameroon	0.8	13.5	14.6	1.1
Algeria	0.6	14.3	15.2	0.9
Mozambique	0.6	18.9	19.7	0.8
Sierra Leone	0.5	11.0	11.7	0.7
Rep. of the Congo	0.4	14.5	15.1	0.6
Lesotho	0.4	30.0	30.6	0.6

Source: Own calculations based on GRD and WDI data

with higher incomes. Third, given that property does not move, they are a stable and predictable source of revenue, which will increase along with development as property and land prices rise. Fourth, they promote accountability, as paying local property taxes increases demand for transparent and efficient public spending on local services. However, as summarised by Ali et al. (2017), a number of factors must be taken into consideration in order to avoid such taxes having unintended consequences. For instance, high taxes on buildings may slow construction of new buildings. Moreover, how properties are valued can affect whether a tax is equitable. Negative outcomes can also arise if the various local tax authorities apply different tax rates, and if enforcement varies significantly between localities.

The trend towards rapid urbanisation in many African countries makes property taxes important. Urban areas are engines of economic growth, and taxing them in an appropriate manner is important if the investment necessary to transform African cities is to be financed. Given this, it may be asked why property taxes are not used more in African countries. The factors are many, but one of the most fundamental barriers to effective property taxation is sustained resistance from property-owning elites, who form a powerful lobby that can block both policy reform and effective implementation (Ali et al., 2017). This problem is particularly evident in large capital cities, where resources are concentrated and political and economic elites tend to be closely linked. Indeed, in such cities, where bureaucratic capacity to overcome some of the administrative challenges is likely to be higher than elsewhere, elite resistance may be the primary obstacle. Other reasons for the poor revenue contribution of property taxes in developing countries include: generally poor administrations; weak enforcement; unclear property rights or poor records of ownership; and the attitude of taxpayers.

Six broad areas can be identified in designing and implementing a property tax system that addresses the various political and administrative challenges outlined above (Collier et al., 2017). First, public support for land and property taxes in cities is linked to tangible benefits arising from public spending, such as improved infrastructure and social services, meaning that a successful strategy must raise awareness among citizens regarding the link between land and/or property taxes, public investment and long-term urban development. Moreover, public authorities must deliver swiftly on promises of better services. Second, if land tenure is not yet formalised, public acceptance of land taxation may be greater if tax reform is linked to a formalisation process. Third, a zero tolerance approach to corruption is key to gaining public support for land and property taxation, and therefore legitimacy. As such, the design and implementation of tax policies must be transparent, publicly accessible and understandable. In addition, administrative procedures should be digitalised, automated and standardised, thereby reducing the potential for corrupt practises. Fourth, taxpayers are more likely to comply with reforms if they are consulted and kept informed during the reform process. Fifth, consolidating the digitised data used for registration, valuation, billing and collection into the same system can improve administrative efficiency at each stage, while reducing the potential for corruption and discretion in the tax system. Sixth, reforms may best be implemented on a city-by-city basis – that is, introduced first in those urban centres where there is robust political support from strong leadership and local taxpayers, with other areas following suit once sufficient political support and capacity have been built up.

In this chapter, we have argued that income tax reform, particularly a move towards taxing individual incomes, is important both in terms of revenue mobilisation and strengthening the social contract between citizens and governments. Building on this, tax systems must be simple and fair, with individuals treated similarly regardless of ethnicity, gender or location. This concept of fairness does not, however, stand in the way of addressing inequalities in the fiscal system at large. In the next chapter, we explore why fiscal systems fail to redistribute.

Road construction in Mozambique. Photo: Victor Brott.

"Moving poorer people up the income distribution scale requires both investment in human capital and an inclusive growth agenda."

Chapter 5, page 57

5. Redistribution: The Role of Taxation and Public Spending

A fiscal system that can successfully translate tax revenues into effective public goods and services provision is an important component of the broader social contract. As such, the question arises of how best to design fiscal systems in support of policies aimed at eliminating poverty and reducing inequality. Specifically, this chapter addresses three key questions. First, do fiscal systems in African countries redistribute? Second, how can fiscal system improve redistribution? And, third, are there limits to the level of redistribution that can be achieved through fiscal systems?

Whether a fiscal system is progressive or not is dependent on how the net impact of tax burdens, as well as access to public services, is distributed across the population. Progressive taxation does not necessarily make a fiscal system progressive, as if the public services delivered are poor (or inaccessible) then the net welfare impact may be regressive, or even impoverish parts of the population. A number of African case studies are available to answer the question of whether fiscal systems are redistributive (Inchauste et al., 2017) – for the purposes of this report, we have selected three that illustrate different outcomes (see Box 2). South Africa is one of the few African countries in which the fiscal system has achieved significant redistribution. By contrast, Ethiopia and Tanzania, which were less unequal to start with, have fiscal systems that redistribute less and/or have an insignificant impact on the poor, even making certain parts of the population poorer.

In terms of redesigning fiscal systems to support redistributive policies, two main avenues are open. First, given that part of the problem is low tax revenue overall, closing the various tax gaps previously highlighted could generate additional revenue that could be directed towards progressive spending. Second, improving efficiency and reallocating public spending can make fiscal systems more progressive.

Trade-offs between revenue mobilisation and redistribution

In rich countries, significant redistribution occurs primarily through using

Box 2. Fiscal incidence in South Africa, Ethiopia and Tanzania

In South Africa, the rich bear the brunt of government redirecting these resources to poorest in society in order to raise their incomes (Inchauste et al., 2017). As a result, the country's fiscal system has lifted some 3.6 million individuals out of poverty (measured as those living on less than USD 2.50 per day in 2005, PPP adjusted). It has also reduced inequality, as can be seen in the Gini coefficient falling from 0.77 before taxes and social spending programmes were applied to 0.59 after their application. On the tax side, the only un-equalising component in the analysis involved excise taxes, with all direct taxes (PIT and payroll taxes) progressive and equalising. Given the latter constitute a relatively high share of GDP, their contribution to reducing the income gap between rich and poor is high. Indirect taxes are neutral, though among them, VAT and the fuel levy are equalising. On the spending side, direct transfers are strongly equalising, with the child support grant and the old-age grant showing the largest marginal contributions to redistribution. Moreover, tertiary education exempted, spending on education is pro-poor (per capita spending declines with income), as is spending on health.

Other African countries, however, redistribute very little, and in some cases the fiscal system makes people poorer. In Ethiopia, fiscal incidence analysis suggests three broad results (Hill et al., 2017). First, the tax and social spending system is equalising overall, with taxes comprising a larger percentage of income for wealthier households, and direct transfers primarily targeting poorer households. Although subsidies are not always progressive, social spending in general is. Second, income taxes and transfers are progressive, and, given their size, help reduce income inequality, as well as the depth and severity of poverty. Third, indirect taxes reduce incomes. When all measured taxes paid and benefits received are incorporated into the analysis, the incidence of extreme poverty can be seen to increase from 31.2% to 32.4%.

In the case of Tanzania, while taxation and social expenditures reduce inequality, the impact on poverty is small (Younger et al., 2016). Overall, the fiscal system reduces inequality, with about half this redistribution the result of very progressive direct taxation. The rest is derived from unusually progressive indirect taxation, and progressive in-kind health and education transfers. This situation implies that taxation in Tanzania is quite effective at redistributing resources away from richer households. The results on the expenditure side of the budget, however, are much less positive, with only one expenditure – the conditional cash transfer (CCT) programme – well targeted at the poor. Moreover, regardless of how well targeted the CCT is, its small scale prevents it from having any significant impact on poverty.

transfer schemes targeted at low-income groups. Thus, the aim of the tax system is to bring in the necessary revenue, which is then redistributed on the spending side. However, in many African countries – as illustrated above in the cases of Ethiopia and Tanzania – low revenue mobilisation prevents countries from scaling up redistributive transfer programmes. Aside from closing income tax gaps, another means of raising additional revenue is VAT, which can generate significant amounts of revenue if applied uniformly, without exemptions.

A critique against removing VAT exemptions is that this will hurt low-income households, as they spend a large proportion of their incomes on exempted products, such as food. While there are conflicting views on whether VATs are regressive or progressive,[25] the additional revenue generated by a particular VAT can then be used to finance progressive spending, thereby achieving a progressive net fiscal effect even in cases where the tax itself is regressive.

Empirical micro-simulation results for four African countries (Ethiopia, Ghana, Senegal, Zambia) suggest that, even when poorer households benefit more in proportional terms, richer households spend significantly more on food and other basic goods in absolute terms, meaning that the exemptions provide them with a much larger implicit cash subsidy (Phillips et al., 2018). Exemptions and reduced rates are costly, with estimates ranging from a little under a quarter of VAT revenues in Ethiopia, to around a third in Senegal and Zambia. Broadening the VAT base could, alongside an untargeted universal basic income, create large net gains for poor households in the four countries studied, in the process reducing inequality and extreme poverty. Moreover, a broad single-rate VAT that generates a significant amount of revenue could also enhance welfare through progressive public spending components (e.g. education, health).

Broadening progressive tax instruments while shrinking spending on less progressive expenditures can make the broader fiscal system more pro-

---

25 Almost all studies that try to evaluate whether a VAT is progressive, regressive or neutral assume that all individuals are affected by VAT regardless of where they purchase their products. A recent analysis of a broad set of countries, which takes into consideration informal consumption, finds that VAT exemptions have no redistributive impact. To avoid resistance when implementing a VAT, however-er, a broadening strategy should coincide with investments in social protection programmes (Bachas et al., 2020).

gressive. For example, how health services are financed in a country affects income inequality, as these services are financed (whether through taxes, insurance premiums or out-of-pocket payments) from household resources. In South Africa, financing universal health coverage through income taxes reduces income inequality, while financing health services through indirect taxes and out-of-pocket health spending has the opposite effect (Ataguba, 2019). There are, though, additional effects that must be considered when income taxes becomes a more important source of taxation. For instance, financing social protection through increased taxes on wages in the formal sector carries the risk of increased unemployment and wage inequality. This can be seen in the case of Ethiopia, where a social security reform contributed to rising wage inequality (Shiferaw et al., 2019). A consumption tax has the advantage of avoiding such unintended effects.

Reallocation of public spending

Governments can also reallocate public spending. A number of African countries have large subsidy programmes for fuel and electricity, which are mostly regressive. In the Tanzanian case, reallocating the electricity subsidy to a progressive expenditure, such as the cash transfer programme, could have a substantial effect on poverty. Governments face trade-offs between different spending patterns, meaning that in some countries it is not the absolute amount of public spending that is the main issue, but its composition and (in)efficiency.[26] Another means of reallocation is open to naturally resource-rich countries, such as oil-rich states in sub-Saharan Africa, where a fraction of oil rents could be transferred to the poor in order to eliminate extreme poverty. The proportion of rents that would need to be transferred varies between countries, ranging from the relatively low (e.g. Angola 6%, Gabon 6%) to the relatively high (e.g. Chad 34%, Nigeria 19%, South Sudan 32%) (Devarajan, 2019). A policy of transferring a significant share of resource rents directly to

---

26 For example, poorly trained teachers and unfilled vacancies in public primary schools have led to very poor performance in basic education. A project covering seven countries in sub-Saharan African shows that for students in these countries the amount of schooling they complete is equivalent to only half the time they spend in school (i.e. eight years in school equates to just four years of schooling), and that after three years of primary public schooling, many lack basic literacy and numeracy skills (Bold et al., 2017). This 'learning crisis' is a state-capability failure, and points to systemic governance, accountability and management issues.

the population, while simultaneously taxing the transfer in order to finance public spending, offers the potential for improving both transparency and legitimacy (Devarajan and Singh, 2012). Citizens would have information about their own wealth, incentivising them to take a greater interest in the efficiency of public spending.

Limits of fiscal policies and long-term investment

Though fiscal policy in South Africa has gone a long way towards achieving redistribution, inequality in the country remains high. As this suggests, there is a limit to what fiscal systems can achieve. Elsewhere, both Botswana and Namibia have been successful in reducing poverty, despite experiencing high income inequality (Figure 13 and Figure 14). In other African countries, fiscal policies have reduced inequality by moving rich people down the scale of income distribution, while doing little to move poorer people up the scale. Thus, as discussed earlier, there is little overall correlation between an African country's tax revenue performance and the degree of inequality and poverty.

13. Income inequality relative to tax revenue (average 2015–2018)

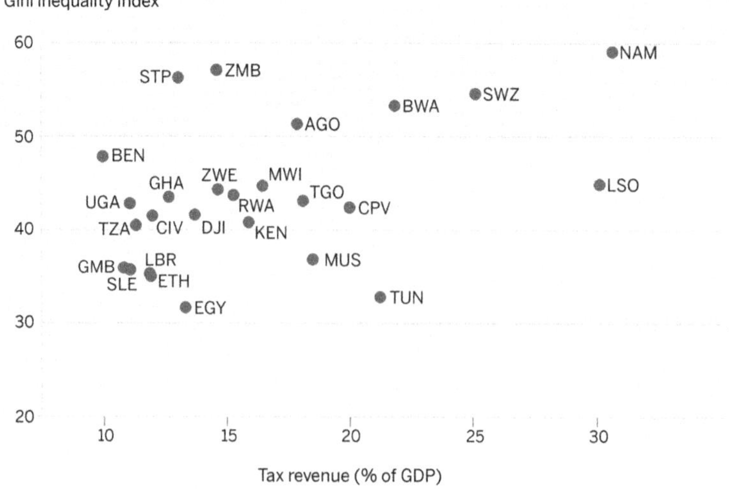

Income inequality is harder to change, as it is determined by the underlying distribution of asset ownership and its change over time. Unequal productive assets (e.g. land, physical and human capital) makes using fiscal policies to compensate for a skewed initial distribution of resources much more difficult. Thus, moving poorer people up the income distribution scale requires both investment in human capital and an inclusive growth agenda that, on top of employment, generates higher productivity at the lower end of the distribution scale.

Addressing these issues and reforming fiscal systems is key to a sustained inclusive development agenda. Also relevant are the wider dynamics of the economic system, particularly in terms of human development and social spending investments. For instance, while education spending represents an

14. Poverty and tax revenue performance (average 2015–2018)

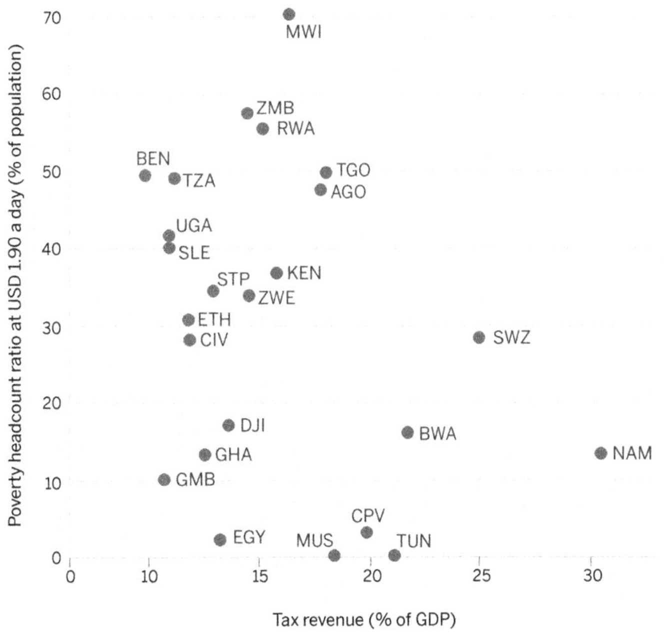

investment in individuals' future income-earning opportunities, it is also an investment in a country's productivity as a whole. Addressing the twin challenges of poverty and inequality in a fiscally sustainable way requires higher, more inclusive economic growth. Such growth is particularly important in addressing the need for more jobs and higher incomes, especially at the lower end of the income distribution. This will, in turn, help narrow the income gap between rich and poor, thereby reinforcing the effectiveness of fiscal policy.

Though public spending affects the accumulation of productive assets, such assets are often not equally distributed geographically. One way of addressing regional inequalities can be seen in current efforts to decentralise public spending functions. However, given tax revenue mobilisation at the local level is often low in African countries, these functions remain highly centralised in the majority of cases, with regions dependent on transfers from national government. Without a fair transparent and system for distributing resource, the risk of such distribution becoming skewed remains.

It is the combination of taxes at a central and local level that ultimately determines the tax burden and, relatedly, compliance.[27] If a tax system has a large number of taxes and/or duplication between the central and local level, taxpayers will find it difficult to determine which taxes to pay. In addition, if an excessive number of taxes is accompanied by different rate structures, the system will become very hard to understand. Reforming tax systems at the central and local level is a comprehensive task that goes beyond the remit of this report. Nevertheless, it is possible to draw some general observations from the literature.[28] In terms of overall tax system design and legislation, consistency between different administrative levels is key. This means the revenue-raising efforts of central and local tax administrations must be streamlined into a single unified system, thereby avoiding double taxation and confusion among taxpayers. Moreover, tax systems at all levels should be consistent with a development agenda focused on employment generation, and should strive for a neutral tax system (i.e. avoiding incentives) that minimises the burden placed on the costs of production. While it may be asserted

---

27 For example, in the Democratic Republic of the Congo, local government laws provide for more than 400 taxes, fees and charges (Moore et al., 2018).

28 For a review of local government taxation in sub-Saharan Africa, see Fjeldstad et al. (2014).

that a fair tax system and redistributive fiscal system are key components of the broader social contract, we currently have little information on whether tax and fiscal systems at the central and local level in African countries are actually fair or redistributive. As such, more in-depth, country-specific analysis is needed, not only in this area but on broader issues such as tax design, legislation and administrative practises.

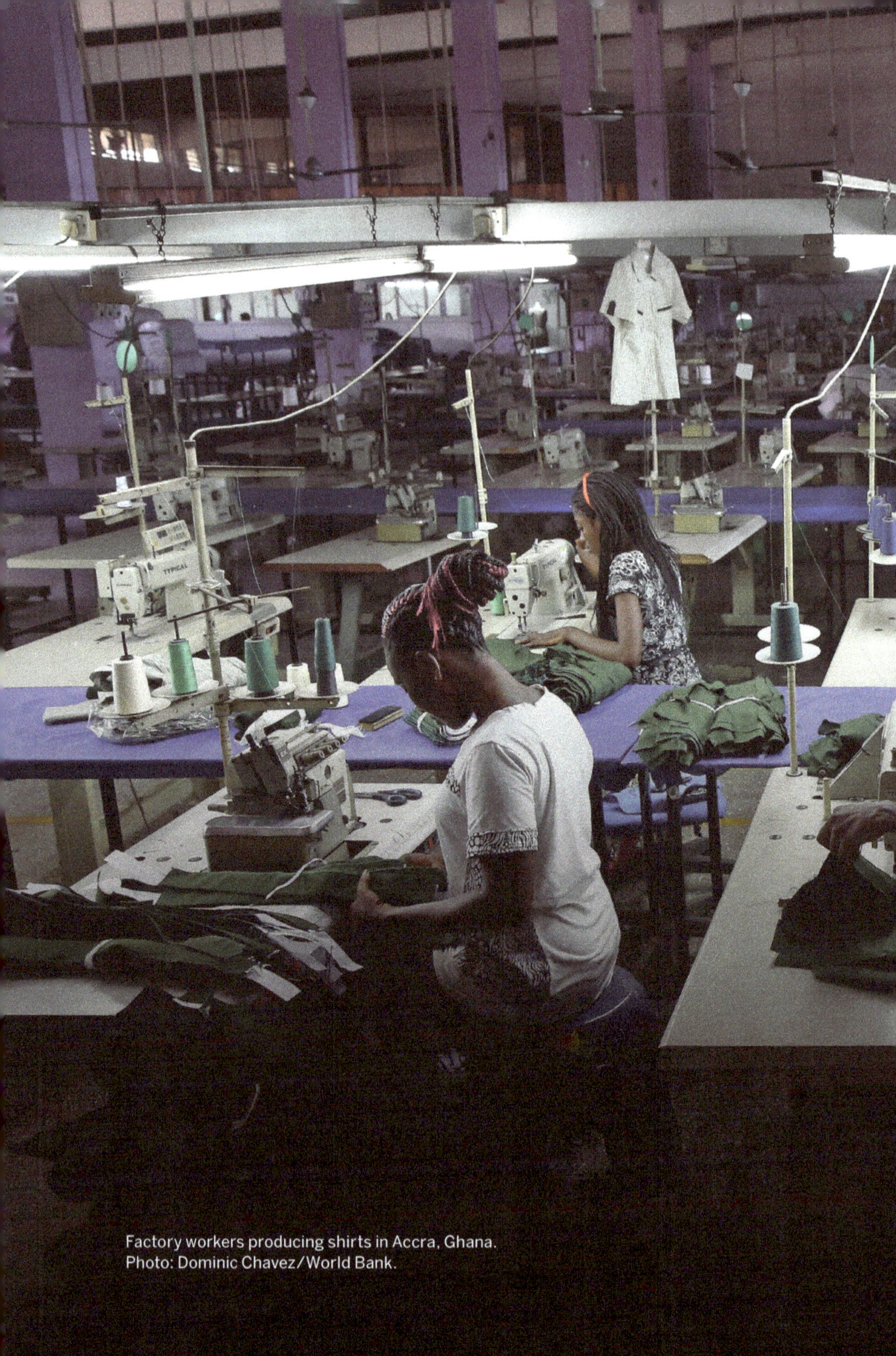

Factory workers producing shirts in Accra, Ghana.
Photo: Dominic Chavez/World Bank.

"A well-designed tax system
can support a structural
transformation process that
includes job creation and
higher incomes."

Chapter 6, page 64

6. Conclusions and Recommendations

Scaling up social protection programmes across Africa has been high on the agenda for some time, with the COVID-19 pandemic now adding impetus when it comes to speeding up this process. Doing so offers the potential for making fiscal systems more equitable. An important factor in why redistribution or poverty reduction often fails to occur is that current social protection programmes remain relatively small. While financing these programmes with domestic tax revenue offers a long-term solution, aggressive short-term tax revenue mobilisation runs the risk of negating their benefits, with individuals potentially paying more in taxes than they receive in transfers and other subsidised services. As such, this report recommends a systematic approach to tax design reform, in order to ensure social protection programmes can be sustained.

While heterogeneity between African countries, both in terms of administrative structure and fiscal capacity, means that tax policy advice must be highly contextualised, there are a number of lessons to be learnt from past successes and mistakes. First, in order to transition towards taxing large tax bases, while simultaneously taking social insurance contributions into consideration, tax systems require reform. To achieve this, the following should be borne in mind:

- **Tax reforms require political commitment and key stakeholder buy-in,** with countries that pursue reforms in both their institutional revenue administration and tax policies tending to see much larger and more persistent gains.
- **Local context matters, and is likely to impact on the sequencing of reforms,** which may include simplifying the tax system; curbing exemptions; reforming indirect taxes on goods and services; and better managing compliance risks by strengthening taxpayer segmentation (often beginning with the large taxpayers office, which includes both large firms and HNWIs).

- **Increased collaboration yields mutual benefits both globally and between African revenue authorities,** particularly when it comes to tackling tax evasion among large (corporate or individual) taxpayers.
- **The overall policy reform agenda requires a medium-term revenue strategy** in order to ensure reform measures are properly sequenced and their implementation facilitated. Even if tax systems change regularly as part of the annual budget process, keeping a tax system's structure intact should be seen as distinct from the process of adjusting tax rates.

Second, this report has highlighted that firms' tax burdens are not equally distributed. Corporate taxation in African countries tends to be low for four reasons. First, tax authorities have failed to register firms that in theory are obliged to pay taxes. Second, a high proportion of firms that are registered are either in the red or reporting zero sales. Third, the tax system's design flaws (generous exemption schemes) mean that the effective tax burden often diverges considerably from statutory rates. Fourth, some multinational enterprises use aggressive tax-planning approaches to reduce their tax payments. The tax burden is also likely to be unfairly distributed between individuals and locations. In addressing these issues, the following should be considered:

- Among many revenue authorities, **there is a need to continue or accelerate the drive to register taxpayers.**
- If the willingness to pay taxes is to be improved, **concerted efforts must be made to improve tax system fairness and the redistributive role of public policies.**
- **A tax system needs to be easily understood** – despite years of reform, individuals in many African countries still have difficulty understanding which taxes they should pay. Thus, ongoing, **long-term tax system reform is needed to develop a unified tax system where the allocation of resources is clear and transparent** across all administrative levels and functions.

Finally, it should be stressed that quick-fix solutions are not conducive to significantly improved tax revenue performance, which must go hand-in-hand with broader development of the economy. In other words, taxation and investment in fiscal capacity will only raise substantial amounts of revenue if they are accompanied by high, sustained economic growth. Many African countries have seen improvements over time, partly due to structural improvements to tax systems made since the 1990s, which have had a tangible impact on how tax revenue responds to economic growth. From a macroeconomic perspective, the way governments tax affects future tax bases, as well as how economies transform themselves structurally. A well-designed tax system can support a structural transformation process that includes job creation and higher incomes. Conversely, poor tax system design can tilt this process towards generating low-paid jobs. Ultimately, whether African countries achieve a demographic dividend depends on which of these two alternatives they choose to take.

References

Ahlerup, P., T. Baskaran and A. Bigsten (2015). 'Tax innovations and public revenues in sub-Saharan Africa'. *The Journal of Development Studies* 51(6): 689–706. Routledge - Taylor and Francis Group.

Akitoby, B., J. Honda, H. Miyamoto, K. Primus and M. Sy (2019). 'Case Studies in Tax Revenue Mobilization in Low-Income Countries'. Working Paper 19/104. Washington, DC: International Monetary Fund.

Ali, M.. O.-H. Fjeldstad and I. Sjursen (2014). 'To pay or not to pay?: Citizens' attitudes towards taxation in Kenya, Tanzania, Uganda and South Africa'. *World Development* 64: 828–842. Elsevier Ltd.

Alstadsæter, A., N. Johannesen and G. Zucman (2017). 'Tax Evasion and Inequality'. Working Paper 23772. Cambridge, MA: National Bureau of Economic Research.

Ataguba, J. (2019). 'Income redistributive effect of taxation and health financing in an unequal society: the case of South Africa'. Paper presented at NAI Workshop 2019.

Bachas. P., L. Gadenne and A. Jensen (2020). 'Informality, Consumption Taxes and Redistribution'. Working Paper 27429. Cambridge, MA: National Bureau of Economic Research.

Bird, R. and E. M. Zolt (2011). 'Dual income taxation: A promising path to tax reform for developing countries'. *World Development* 39(10): 1691–1703. Elsevier Ltd.

Bold, T., D. Filmer, G. Martin, E. Molina, C. Rockmore, B. Stacy, J. Svensson and W. Wane (2017). 'What Do Teachers Know and Do? Does It Matter? Evidence from Primary Schools in Africa'. Policy Research Working Paper 7956. Washington, DC: World Bank.

Carreras, M., C. Dachapalli and G. Mascagni (2017). 'Effective corporate tax burden and firm size in South Africa.' WIDER Working Paper No. 2017/162.

Chuku, C., U. Ibanga and A. Iriabije (2019). 'Tax Compliance by African Businesses: What Matters and What Doesn't'. Paper presented at NAI Workshop 2019.

Cobham, A. and P. Jansky (2018). 'Global distribution of revenue loss from corporate tax avoidance: Re-estimation and country results'. *Journal of International Development* 30(2): 206–232. John Wiley & Sons, Ltd.

Collier, P., E. Glaeser, T. Venables, P. Manwaring and M. Blake (2017). 'Land and Property Taxes: Exploiting Untapped Municipal Revenues'. Policy Brief. International Growth Centre.

Devarajan, S. (2019). 'How to use oil revenues efficiently'. In: K. Mohaddes, J. B. Nugent and H. Selim (eds.), *Institutions and Macroeconomic Policies in Resource-Rich Arab Economies*. Oxford University Press.

Devarajan, S. and R. Singh (2012). 'Government failure and poverty reduction in the CEMAC'. In: B. Akitoby and S. Coorey (eds.), *Oil Wealth in Central Africa: Policies for Inclusive Growth*. Washington, DC: International Monetary Fund.

Efobi U., I. Beecroft and T. Belmondo (2019). 'Small Business Use of the Integrated Tax Administration System in Nigeria'. African Tax Administration Paper 8. Brighton: International Centre for Tax and Development.

Fjeldstad, O-H., G. Chambas and J. F. Brun (2014). 'Local Government Taxation in Sub-Saharan Africa: A Review and an Agenda for Research'. Working Paper WP 2014: 2. CMI/ICTD.

Fjeldstad, O-H., C. Kagoma,, E. Mdee, H. Sjursen and V. Somville (2020). 'The customer is king: Evidence on VAT compliance in Tanzania'. *World Development* 128. Elsevier Ltd.

Gaspar, V., L. Jaramillo and P. Wingender (2016). 'Tax Capacity and Growth: Is there a Tipping Point?' Working Paper WP/16/234. Fiscal Affairs Department. Washington, DC: International Monetary Fund.

Hill, R., G. Inchauste, N. Lustig, E. Tsehaye and T. Woldehanna (2017). 'Fiscal incidence analysis for Ethiopia'. In: G. Inchauste and N. Lustig (eds.), *The Distributional Impact of Taxes and Transfers Evidence from Eight Low- and Middle-Income Countries*. IBRD/World Bank.

Inchauste, G., N. Lustig, M. Maboshe, C. Purfield and I. Woolard (2017). 'The distributional impact of fiscal policy in South Africa'. In: G. Inchauste, and N. Lustig (eds.), *The Distributional Impact of Taxes and Transfers Evidence from Eight Low- and Middle-Income Countries*. IBRD/World Bank.

Joshi, A., W. Prichard and C. Heady (2014). 'Taxing the informal economy: The current state of knowledge and agendas for future research'. *The Journal of Development Studies* 50(10): 1325–1347. Routledge – Taylor and Francis Group.

Jouste M., M. I. Nalukwago and R. Waiswa (2019). 'Do Tax Administrative Interventions Targeted to Small Businesses Improve Tax Compliance and Revenue Collection? Evidence from Ugandan Tax Administrative Data'. Working Paper. UNU/WIDER.

Kanbur, R. (2017). 'Informality: Causes, consequences and policy responses'. *Review of Development Economics* 21(4): 939–961. John Wiley & Sons, Ltd.

Kangave, J., S. Nakato, R. Waiswa and P. L. Zzimbe (2016). 'Boosting Revenue Collection through Taxing High Net Worth Individuals: The Case of Uganda'. Working Paper 45. Brighton: International Centre for Tax and Development.

Keen, M. and M. Mansour (2009). 'Revenue Mobilization in Sub-Saharan Africa: Challenges from Globalization'. Working Paper WP/09/157. Washington, DC: International Monetary Fund.

Lofgren, H. and M. Cicowiez (2019). 'Taxation, Infrastructure Investment, Growth, and Poverty Reduction: A Case Study of Zimbabwe'. Paper presented at NAI Workshop 2019.

Löffler, G., T. Strauss and B. Welham (2018). 'Strengthening Taxation and Tax Auditing of the Mining Sector: Lessons Learnt From Four West African Countries'. Deutsche Gesellschaft für Internationale Zusammenarbeit (GIZ) GmbH.

Mascagni, G. and A. T. Mengistu (2016). 'The Corporate Tax Burden in Ethiopia: Evidence from Anonymised Tax Returns'. Working Paper 48. Brighton: International Centre for Tax and Development.

Masiyandima, N. and Mlambo (2018). Tax Revenue Productivity and Economic Informality in Zimbabwe. Paper presented at NAI Workshop 2019.

Mkandawire, T. (2010). 'On Tax efforts and colonial heritage in Africa'. *The Journal of Development Studies* 46(10): 1647–1669. Routledge – Taylor and Francis Group.

Moore, M., P. Prichard and O-H. Fjeldstad (2018). *Taxing Africa: Coercion, Reform and Development*. London: Zed Books.

Ndung'u, N. (2019). 'Taxing Mobile Phone Transactions in Africa: Lessons from Kenya'. Brookings Africa Growth Initiative Policy Brief.

Phillips, D., R. Warwick, M. Goldman, K. Goraus, G. Inchauste, T. Harris and J. Jellema (2018). 'Redistribution via VAT and Cash Transfers: An Assessment in Four Low and Middle Income Countries', Commitment to Equity (CEQ) Working Paper Series 78. Tulane University, Department of Economics.

Prichard W., A. Custers, R. Dom, S. Davenport and M. Roscitt (2019). 'Innovations in Tax Compliance Conceptual Framework'. Policy Research Working Paper 9032. Washington, DC: World Bank.

Rogers, M. and X. Pedros (2017). 'Taxing Mobile Connectivity in Sub-Saharan Africa: A Review of Mobile Sector Taxation and its Impact on Digital Inclusion'. Available at: www.gsma.com/mobilefordevelopment/wp-content.

Shiferaw, A., M. Söderbom, A. Bedi and G. Alemu (2019). 'Wage Growth and Social Security Reform'. GLM|LIC Working Paper 45.

Shimeles, A., D. Z. Gurara and F. Woldeyes (2017). 'Taxman's dilemma: Coercion or persuasion? Evidence from a randomized field experiment in Ethiopia'. *American Economic Review: Papers & Proceedings* 107(5): 420–424. American Economic Association.

Suri, T. and W. Jack (2016). 'The Long-run poverty and gender impacts of mobile money'. *Science* 354(6317): 1288–1292. DOI: 10.1126/science.aah5309.

Waiswa, R., M. I. Nalukwago, J. Kangave, S. Nakato and L. P. Zzimbe (2017). 'Taxing High Net Worth Individuals in Uganda Phase 1&2'. Powerpoint presentation, ICTD.

Wier, L. (2020). 'Tax-motivated transfer mispricing in South Africa: Direct evidence using transaction data'. *Journal of Public Economics* 184. Elsevier Ltd.

World Bank (2015). 'Why Should Tanzanians Pay Taxes? The Unavoidable Need to Finance Economic Development'. Tanzania Economic Update Issue 7. Washington, DC: World Bank.

World Bank (2020). *The African Continental Free Trade Area: Economic and Distributional Effects*. International Bank for Reconstruction and Development. Washington, DC: World Bank.

Yohou, H. D. and M. Goujon (2017). 'Reassessing Tax Effort in Developing Countries: A Proposal of a Vulnerability-Adjusted Tax Effort Index (VATEI)'. Working Paper 186. Fondation pour les études et recherches sur le développement international.

Younger, S. D., F. Myamba and K. Mdadila (2016). 'Fiscal incidence in Tanzania'. *African Development Review* 28(3): 264–276. John Wiley & Sons, Ltd.

Appendix 1:
ISO Codes and Countries

AGO	Angola	MAR	Morocco
BDI	Burundi	MDG	Madagascar
BEN	Benin	MLI	Mali
BFA	Burkina Faso	MOZ	Mozambique
BWA	Botswana	MRT	Mauritania
CAF	Central African Republic	MUS	Mauritius
CIV	Cote d'Ivoire	MWI	Malawi
CMR	Cameroon	NAM	Namibia
COD	Democratic Republic of the Congo	NER	Niger
COG	Republic of the Congo	NGA	Nigeria
COM	Comoros	RWA	Rwanda
CPV	Cape Verde	SDN	Sudan
DJI	Djibouti	SEN	Senegal
DZA	Algeria	SLE	Sierra Leone
EGY	Egypt	SOM	Somalia
ERI	Eritrea	SSD	South Sudan
ETH	Ethiopia	STP	Sao Tome and Principe
GAB	Gabon	SWZ	Eswatini
GHA	Ghana	SYC	Seychelles
GIN	Guinea	TCD	Chad
GMB	The Gambia	TGO	Togo
GNB	Guinea-Bissau	TUN	Tunisia
GNQ	Equatorial Guinea	TZA	Tanzania
KEN	Kenya	UGA	Uganda
LBR	Liberia	ZAF	South Africa
LBY	Libya	ZMB	Zambia
LSO	Lesotho	ZWE	Zimbabwe